The Up-to-Date Presentation of the God-Ordained Way

and the Signs Concerning the Coming of Christ

Witness Lee

Living Stream Ministry
Anaheim, CA

First Edition, January 1991.

ISBN 978-0-87083-564-3

Published by

Living Stream Ministry
2431 W. La Palma Ave., Anaheim, CA 92801 U.S.A.
P. O. Box 2121, Anaheim, CA 92814 U.S.A.

Printed in the United States of America

09   10   11   12   13   14   /   12   11   10   9   8   7   6   5   4   3

CONTENTS

PREFACE

This book is composed of messages given by Brother Witness Lee in Malaysia from October 24 through November 6, 1990. Chapter one is a message given in Kota Kinabalu concerning the proper Christian meetings and services. Chapters two and three contain messages given in Kuching on the recovery of the God-ordained way. Chapters four and five contain messages given in Petaling Jaya concerning the New Testament priestly service. Chapters six and seven contain messages given in Kuching concerning the coming of Christ and the consummation of the age. The original messages were spoken in Chinese.

CHAPTER ONE

THE RECOVERY
OF THE PROPER CHRISTIAN
MEETING AND SERVICE

Whenever we the believers meet, we have three precious things. First, we have the Lord's name. The Lord said that whenever we are gathered into His name, He is in our midst (Matt. 18:20). Therefore, whenever we come together, we should believe that the Lord is with us. His name is our enjoyment. Second, we have the Lord's Spirit. The Lord's Spirit is with us all the time and everywhere, but when we meet together, the Lord's Spirit is doubly present with us. Third, we have the Lord's word. Whenever we meet, we have the Lord's speaking to us. Furthermore, these three things— the Lord's name, the Lord's Spirit, and the Lord's word—are the Lord Himself. When we draw a deep breath by calling, "O Lord Jesus," we feel refreshed in our body and clear in our heart. This is neither a superstition nor something of our imagination; it is God Himself coming into us to be our supply.

THE INFLUENCE
OF TRADITIONAL CHRISTIANITY

I would like to tell you a little about our history. Up to the present time, the Lord's recovery has been among us for almost seventy years. The first meeting was started in 1922 in Foochow by Brother Watchman Nee and others. Brother Nee was the first to bring in the Lord's recovery, whereas I was the one who raised up the first church among us in the north, in my hometown, Chefoo, in 1932. Brother Nee and I both came out from the background of Christianity. Brother

Nee's grandfather was a pastor, and my mother was a third generation Christian. We were alike in that we were born in Christianity, we grew up in Christianity, and we were educated in Christianity. Therefore, it was not easy for us to escape the influence of Christianity. At that time we were still young. It was an unstable time—the country was segmented by the warlords, the government was corrupt, and the people were suffering. Seeing the international situation and considering the future of the country, many young people really desired to do something. At that time the Lord did a particular work in China and raised up a number of young people who loved the Lord and who lived for the Lord. They were all our age. However, after a time most of them did not take the way of the Lord's recovery. By the Lord's mercy, we remained. We surely saw the revelation of the Lord and knew the deviation of Christianity. Therefore, we determined to have only three things—the Bible, the Lord's name, and salvation; the rest we could do without.

Although we had made such a determination, there was still the question of how we should meet. From our childhood we had not seen any kind of meeting outside Christianity; we had already seen enough of the whole order of things in Christianity. Therefore, when we desired to meet, naturally it was difficult for us to be rid of the "color" of the denominations. I can still remember that when I was twenty-six or twenty-seven years old, a meeting was raised up in my mother's home, and I took the lead there. Although I had not studied in a seminary, nor had I been a pastor or a preacher, I had to give a message and lead the prayer. Therefore, the way of meeting in Christianity was spontaneously brought over to our meetings. In October of 1933, after I gave up my job, I went to Shanghai to see Brother Nee, and I stayed there. I very much appreciated some of the things that I noticed in the way they met that we did not practice in the north. However, for the most part, their way was about the same as ours: someone led the meeting, someone gave a message, someone concluded the meeting, and all the rest listened to the message. It was always like this.

THE RECOVERY OF
PRAYING OVER THE HYMNS,
PRAY-READING THE LORD'S WORD,
CALLING ON THE LORD'S NAME,
AND SPEAKING THE HYMNS TO ONE ANOTHER

In 1949 I was sent to work abroad, first to Taiwan, and the next year to the Philippines. Probably in 1953 or 1954, we began to practice praying over the hymns; that is, after singing a hymn, the brothers and sisters would utter some prayers according to the hymn. Everybody felt that this was very enjoyable, and as a result everyone became living. Ten years later, I went to the United States. Then in 1966 I returned to Taiwan, and it was at that time that the saints in Tainan began to practice pray-reading, joining the reading of the Word with prayer, that is, not only reading but also praying. Because of this, many saints were released, and the situation became very flourishing. This practice spread rapidly to San Francisco, and when the saints there received it, they too were benefitted. Thus, we have the praying over the hymns and the pray-reading of the Lord's Word. One time, before the Lord's Day morning meeting, while everyone was sitting quietly and waiting, as was our custom, I stood up and said, "Everyone who came to the meeting can say four words." As I was speaking, I still did not know what the four words were. While I was speaking, I was considering. Then I spoke the following four words: "O Lord, Amen, Hallelujah!" Everyone practiced this on the spot, and some immediately composed some songs concerning it. Then this became prevailing. I knew that this was the Lord's leading. So at that point we added another item—calling on the Lord's name. At that time we were meeting in Elden Hall in Los Angeles. Many saints had moved to the neighborhood of the meeting hall. In the early evening, one could hear the voices of the saints calling, "O Lord Jesus!" Everyone was calling—calling in the homes, calling on the streets, and calling in the meeting hall. That fervent situation lasted for a considerable time. In 1968 I was invited to Jakarta, Indonesia. In a meeting there, I spoke concerning Ephesians 5:19, which says that we can speak to one another in psalms. Out of this came the speaking of the hymns one to another. As a result, the meetings became even more living than before.

MEETINGS THAT ARE
LIVING AND HAVE THE SPIRIT

I hope that we all can be clear that we Christians have God with us. God's presence is like the air. Thus, we do not need to seek for any feeling. The more any matter is related to life, the more it needs to be normal. The thing we need the most is air, yet our breathing is a very ordinary thing, without any special feeling. The more experience I have, the more I sense that our spiritual life is similar to our physical life—the more normal it is, the fewer problems there are, and the less need there is for any feeling. After we finish eating a meal, digestion begins to take place in our stomach, yet we do not feel it at all. If we feel something, that is a sign that there is something wrong. The more we regularly experience the spiritual things, the richer we become, yet there is no spectacular sensation. Now we are gathered here into the Lord's name. Although we do not particularly sense the Lord's presence, we have to admit that the Lord is with us. His being with us is like the air's being with us. The Lord's name is the Lord Himself. When we are gathered into the Lord's name, we come into the Lord's presence.

Therefore, I hope that from this day on in our gatherings, no one would wait. Once we come into a meeting, we should call on the Lord, praise the Lord, and begin to pray. When someone begins and another continues, the meeting begins. Some may pray, some may call hymns, and some may testify. Whoever comes into the meeting first should begin the meeting. Then those who come later should continue. As more and more people come, the meeting will become richer and richer. There are no forms or rituals, for the letter kills (2 Cor. 3:6b). The letter refers to the ordinances of the Old Testament law. The Old Testament is the age of the law. What the Old Testament speaks about is just the law. But when we come to the New Testament, nothing is of the law, but everything is a matter of the Spirit. Hence, whenever we meet, our meeting must be living and must have the Spirit.

A SERVICE THAT IS EFFECTIVE

I would like to speak concerning another matter. Formerly, when we were leading people to salvation, we first considered them as seeking friends. After hearing the gospel and believing and receiving the Lord, they had to successfully pass through an interview concerning baptism. It was only after they had passed the interview that they could be baptized and saved. Now we have changed. As long as a person believes, he can be baptized immediately, and he is regenerated and saved. Furthermore, the Bible says, "He who believes and is baptized shall be saved" (Mark 16:16). It does not say that one is baptized after he is saved. Baptism is not carried out after a person is saved; baptism is part of the process of being saved. It is not that one believes and is saved and therefore should be baptized. Rather, it is that one believes and is baptized and therefore is saved. We must be clear concerning this matter.

Moreover, we have tried many ways in the Lord's recovery related to the preaching of the gospel for fruit bearing. Thus far I can say that the most effective way is not merely to love the Lord and have a heart to save souls, but to be revived every morning and to overcome daily. To have a morning revival means that every morning, following the sequence in the Bible, you use two or three verses of the Word to enjoy the Lord not only by reading, but even more by praying. You should not merely read, nor should you pray with your own words. Rather, you should turn the words in the Bible into your prayer to the Lord. In this way you will receive a supply, and your entire being will be revived. This is like the sun rising again every day to re-enliven all things. This is a law of life. Then, based on such a revival, during the whole day you will have these few enjoyable verses of Scripture in you as your sustaining strength for the supply of your daily walk. Then you will overcome daily.

After you experience the morning revival and the daily overcoming, you will receive the burden to preach the gospel. Whether or not you have the opportunity, you will preach the gospel. You can make a list of the names of twenty of your relatives, colleagues, classmates, and neighbors, and pray for them. These are "warm doors" for you to visit. You also may coordinate with other saints to preach to those who have not yet believed, even though you have been contacting them for a long time. Moreover, you may also bring them to the group meetings to give them the opportunity to contact others and listen to testimonies. Then, you may preach the gospel to them individually and exercise the Lord's authority to lead them to believe in Christ, to call on the Lord's name, and to be baptized and be saved. After their baptism, you should give them a lesson to show them that today the Lord is the Spirit dwelling in them. You need to teach them how to exercise their spirit to call on the Lord's name at any time and to pray to Jesus in everything. Then you may make an appointment with them to call them every morning to have a morning revival, and you may also tell them that from that night on they should read one chapter of the Bible every night before they go to bed. After you have led someone to salvation, he becomes a child begotten by you through the gospel. Therefore, you need to take care of him and nourish him. You need to visit him personally every three to five days. You should be concerned about him and supply him with life and lead him on. After you continue to do this for two or three months, he will become a remaining fruit, one who remains in the church life.

I hope that after hearing this kind of speaking, every one of you will mean business to practice it and do it in a thorough way. If you really do this, the church will increase yearly and will be full of riches and glory.

(A message given by Brother Witness Lee in Kota Kinabalu, Malaysia on October 24, 1990)

CHAPTER TWO

THE RECOVERY OF THE GOD-ORDAINED WAY

(1)

Prayer: Lord, You are the One whom we seek; we know that You are concealed in Your holy Word. We pray that You will release Yourself from Your Word. We all desire to hear You, to see You, and to gain something from You. Lord, we place ourselves before You to receive Your enlightenment and penetration. We pray that You will expose our true condition, that in Your light we may know ourselves as we know You. Amen.

GOD'S ORIGINAL INTENTION—
THAT EVERYONE BE A PRIEST

In this meeting I would like to fellowship with you concerning several portions of the Word which are very fundamental and practical, and with which we need to check our service and work today, that we may be clear about the way to go on.

Romans 15:16 says, "So that I might be a minister of Christ Jesus to the Gentiles, a laboring priest of the gospel of God, in order that the offering of the Gentiles might be acceptable, having been sanctified in the Holy Spirit." To labor is to not be lazy but to be industrious; it includes striving, expending great effort, and endeavoring to go on by struggling. This can be likened to the endeavoring of the ancient Greek Olympic athletes. Unfortunately, most of the English versions do not include the word "laboring"; some render this portion only as "serving as a priest of the gospel of God." We know that all New Testament believers are priests, but five years ago we did not point out what the New Testament priests do. What the priests of the Old Testament did was mostly to offer sacrifices and handle the offerings, but what do the priests of the New Testament do?

THE PRODUCING OF THE PRIESTLY TRIBE OF LEVI

In Exodus 19 God called the children of Israel, saying, "Now therefore, if ye will obey my voice indeed, and keep my covenant, then ye shall be a peculiar treasure unto me above all people: for all the earth is mine: and ye shall be unto me a kingdom of priests, and a holy nation" (vv. 5-6a). In the beginning, God's ordination was that all the people of Israel would be priests. However, not long after that, they worshipped the golden calf and blasphemed God. This caused Moses to shatter the stone tablets and to charge the people to stand on God's side and slay their brothers. At that time, only the Levites did as Moses had asked (32:25-29). Then, in Deuteronomy 33:8-9 God blessed Levi through Moses, saying, "May Your Thummim and Urim be with Your godly man...he who said of his father and mother, I do not regard him; and his brothers he did not acknowledge, and his children he did not recognize; for they have kept Your speaking and have guarded Your covenant." From then on, only the Levites could be priests, and a nation of priests became a tribe of priests. Furthermore, only the house of Aaron could be priests; the rest of the Levites were only the serving ones. Then, in Numbers 16 the rebellion of Korah and his company took place because they were not content to remain in a secondary position in the service. So Moses rebuked them, saying, "Hear now, you sons of Levi: Is it too small a thing for you that the God of Israel has separated you from the assembly of Israel to bring you near to Himself, to do the service of the tabernacle of Jehovah, and to stand before the assembly to minister to them...And will you seek the priesthood also?" (vv. 8-10). This shows that the children of Israel in the Old Testament were divided into three classes: the priesthood of the house of Aaron, the serving Levites, and the common people.

THE FORMATION OF THE CLERGY-LAITY SYSTEM
AND THE RAISING UP OF THE LORD'S RECOVERY

However, in the New Testament, all the believers in the

church are priests. This takes us back to God's original intention. After the passing away of the early apostles, people gradually became unclear concerning the service rendered to God; thus, the teaching concerning the "clergy-laity" came forth. First, Ignatius in the second century taught that an overseer, a bishop, is higher than an elder. From this erroneous teaching came the religious organization of bishops, archbishops, cardinals, and the pope. This teaching is also the source of the episcopal system of ecclesiastical government. Then, in A.D. 590, the archbishop of Rome was recognized by the Eastern and Western churches as the pope; thus, the Roman Catholic Church was officially formed. Later, after further gradual development, there came to be not only bishops, each governing a district, but also archbishops, each having jurisdiction mainly over a country. Then, still higher in rank are the cardinals, who surround the pope to rule over all the Catholic churches on the whole globe, and thus may be considered the pope's cabinet members. If the pope dies, the cardinals elect a new pope from among themselves. In the sixteenth century, Martin Luther rose up to make reforms; as a result, the Protestant churches came into being from the Catholic Church. In the early stage, the Protestant churches were state churches in nature. A number of the northern European countries began to form state churches, such as the Anglican Church, also known as the Episcopalian Church in England, and the Lutheran Church in Germany. The kings of the states became the leaders of the state churches. This way of governing the churches was the same as the practice in the Catholic Church. A century later, in approximately 1690, some saw the truth concerning the church being governed by the elders, not the bishops; as a result, the Presbyterian Church was established. This was the beginning of the independent churches. After this, some saw the truth concerning baptism by immersion (instead of by sprinkling), so they formed the Baptist Church. After this, there was a gradual recovery of the church, but in the matter of service, the church still could not escape the influence of the clergy-laity system.

In the seventeenth century, the Moravian brothers were

raised up. Because of the persecution from the Catholic Church, the state churches, and the independent churches, the brothers fled to the estate of Brother Zinzendorf. From that point on, the recovery of the church life began. In 1828 some brothers rose up in England. They broke away from all their background and lived and served altogether according to the truth of the Bible; they did not deny the Lord's name, and they kept the Lord's word. Unfortunately, after no more than half a century, they became degraded. Then, in 1922 the Lord raised us up in the Far East. In the beginning, we adopted mainly the practices of the Brethren. Later, we discovered that in a considerable number of areas we had not entered deeply enough into the biblical truths. First, in 1934 Brother Nee released the book entitled *The Meeting Life,* in which he spoke concerning the establishing of the elders and the governing of the church. In 1948 he published the book entitled *Church Affairs* in which he pointed out emphatically that the traditional meeting on the Lord's Day, like the following of the customs of the nations by the children of Israel in the Old Testament (2 Kings 17:8), was abominable to God. Therefore, he said, we should push it out so that everyone can function. However, because the traditional way of meeting had become a firmly established habit and custom among mankind and had penetrated into the very blood of Christians, it could not be uprooted instantly. Later, the Lord's recovery went to Taiwan. Because the time was not ripe to have a change, we went on according to the old practices; after about thirty years, we gradually slipped back to the condition that presently exists in Christianity, and we came to a standstill.

I hope you all can see what the Lord's recovery is. Beginning from the Brethren, the Lord's recovery first was the recovery of the oneness of the Body of Christ; then it was the eliminating of all the practices that are not scriptural. Hence, we broke away from the denominations, and we desired to have only the Lord's name and the Lord's word. We wanted only Christ and the church and did not want any division. The more we went on with the Lord, the more we discovered that in our service and meetings, our practice was

not absolutely according to the Lord's Word. We realized that
we did not begin in an absolute way; we merely inherited
the ways of the past, so that the more we practiced them, the
more they proved to be unworkable, and the more problems
we had.

The Lord did bless His recovery, so that by 1984 there
were eight or nine hundred churches raised up on the whole
earth, covering the six major continents. However, unconsciously we fell into a condition in which there was a lack;
that is, our inner life was not sufficiently fresh and living. All
the churches, in both the east and in the west, were in a
dormant state, in a condition like that of Sardis. Moreover,
the increase in the number of believers was very slow. Among
the churches in the United States, for example, from 1962 to
1977 the yearly rate of increase was close to thirty percent,
which is probably something very rare in church history.
Later, because of the attack by the slandering ones, the church
was affected. From 1977 to 1984, the rate of increase of the
believers was no more than two or three percent yearly. In
October of that year, after I finished the last life-study of the
New Testament, I determined to go back to Taipei to thor-
oughly restudy this matter.

THE RECOVERY OF SOME IMPORTANT WORDS
OF THE SCRIPTURES

After six years of study, I discovered some passages in the
holy Word that we had altogether neglected. The first is
Romans 15:16 concerning the priests of the gospel. We have
said that all believers should preach the gospel and that all
are priests; but in practice we still have the clerical class in
that only a few are functioning in this way. The second
passage is 1 Corinthians 14:26. More than forty years ago
Brother Nee saw the matter mentioned in this verse and
spoke concerning it, but up to the present time we have not
practiced it. The third portion is Ephesians 4:11-16, which
says that the Lord has given some gifts to the church unto the
work of the ministry, unto the building up of His Body. These
gifted persons need to perfect the saints, and then the saints
will be able to do what the gifted persons do and will properly

function. In this way the entire Body grows gradually and is built up organically. The fourth portion is John 15:16. There the Lord said, "You did not choose Me, but I chose you, and I appointed you that you should go forth and bear fruit, and that your fruit should remain." As we enjoy Christ as grace and as our life, the result will be that we will bear remaining fruit. Then, another passage is John 21:15-17, which says that the fruit we bear becomes the flock under our shepherding. Finally, Hebrews 10:24-25 says, "And let us consider one another for inciting to love and good works, not forsaking the assembling of ourselves together, as the custom with some is, but exhorting one another." This kind of meeting, in which we consider one another and exhort one another, refers to the group meeting. We must admit that we have not been properly practicing what is taught in the aforementioned verses.

THE STEPS FOR THE OFFERING OF SACRIFICES BY THE NEW TESTAMENT PRIESTS OF THE GOSPEL

We have said that the main work of the priests is to offer sacrifices. However, the sacrifices offered by the New Testament priests are absolutely different from the sacrifices offered by the Old Testament priests. In the Old Testament, the priests offered bulls and goats, but in the New Testament, the priests offer as sacrifices those who have been saved into Christ and who are joined to Christ. The bulls and goats as sacrifices in the Old Testament are types of the coming Christ (Heb. 10:5-7); but the redeemed sinners are in the Christ who has come, and they have become members of the Body of Christ. They are presented to God by the New Testament priests of the gospel as living and spiritual sacrifices. First Peter 2:5 says that we are "living stones, being built up a spiritual house, into a holy priesthood, to offer up spiritual sacrifices acceptable to God through Jesus Christ." This shows that the intention of God's heart is to have a spiritual house for Him to dwell in and to have a priestly body, a priesthood, to serve Him. As priests, we serve corporately in coordination to "tell out the virtues of Him who has called you out of darkness into His marvelous light," as mentioned in

2:9, that we may offer up spiritual sacrifices acceptable to God, that is, saved sinners, according to God's economy. Therefore, we need to realize that to preach the gospel is to tell out God's love, grace, forgiveness, redemption, and so forth, that we may bring sinners to the Lord and offer them, the members of Christ, as sacrifices to God. This is the first step of the priests' offering of sacrifices.

The second step of the offering of sacrifices is to nourish the believers that they may grow in life so that they can present themselves as sacrifices to God. Romans 12:1 speaks of this. We should beseech the believers through the compassions of God that they may offer themselves as a living sacrifice to God. The third step is that we who are priests should do according to what Paul said in Colossians 1:28-29, that is, warn every man and teach every man in all wisdom, that we may present every man to God full-grown in Christ. This requires us to labor and to struggle. All that we have is Christ, and all that we offer also is Christ (cf. 1 Cor. 14:26 and note 1). Only by doing this can we be the priests of the gospel.

THE WAY TO BE THE NEW TESTAMENT PRIESTS OF THE GOSPEL

Since we are priests of the gospel, we need to preach the gospel to save sinners. Since we are branches of the Lord, we need to bear fruit. In the past we practiced "preaching the gospel by the church," meaning that everyone took part in preaching the gospel, and the effect was not bad. However, we did not reach the level of being priests of the gospel. Since every believer is a New Testament priest of the gospel, everyone needs to preach the gospel to offer saved sinners as sacrifices to God. This is the service that is according to the Scriptures. For this reason, since 1984 we have seen the need to change our practice. In the past six years, we were continually experimenting and trying out various ways, and did not have a definite way of practice. From 1984 we had some realization, and in August 1986 a training center was formally established in Taipei as the laboratory to research the God-ordained new way. It was not until August of last year that I felt that we had found a definite way; we have finished the preliminary step of the study of the new way and have something to present to the churches.

First, every church must receive grace from the Lord to stir up and motivate the brothers and sisters to build up the habit of contacting people, and the best way to contact people is to knock on "warm doors." Every brother and sister should make a list of twenty names that includes their unsaved relatives, friends, classmates, colleagues, and neighbors. The people on the list will serve as the objects for the saints to contact in their preaching of the gospel in mutual coordination. Some relatives whom you have been contacting for years are still not saved. But the result might be different if someone else preaches to them, and it is possible that they will be saved. There are many examples of those who have been saved in such a way. There are over one thousand three hundred churches in the Lord's recovery on the whole earth. If every church has fifty priests of the gospel who go out to contact the acquaintances of all the saints, the gospel will spread.

Next, group meetings must be established in all the places. To properly practice the group meetings, we must be living and organic. There are no set ways to have group meetings, and to have such a meeting is not to have a "worship service." Group meetings are for free fellowship, prayer, and mutual care and shepherding. In the meeting there is no program, no schedule, and no one who takes the lead. On our way to the meeting, we should begin to praise and sing. When we arrive at the brother or sister's home, we should not wait but should begin to fellowship and share, sing, or pray, doing everything according to the Spirit. If there is a need, we should pray for one another and care for one another. We can also tell one another about our present condition and can nourish one another. At the same time, we should also carry out some teaching of the truth. This is not to have some specially appointed ones do the teaching, but to have the mutual asking of questions and mutual teaching. In this way all the individual fellowships will add up to a very good message; this will render help to the attendants. This kind of practice still needs our deeper study.

For the practice of the new way, first we must be revived every morning, and then we must have an overcoming daily life. Every day we should rise up early to call on the Lord's name and have fellowship with the Lord. Then we should get into His Word and use two or three verses to enjoy Him. This will enable us to have a new beginning with the Lord in the morning. After this, to serve as a reminder, we may jot down the points concerning which the Lord inspired us with when we were with Him. When the weekend comes, we can put together the inspirations of the six days and compose a very good draft of a prophecy with which we can prophesy for the Lord in the Lord's Day meeting. We should not only do this ourselves, but we should also perfect others to do this so that more saints will be able to function. Thus the meetings will surely be fresh, rich, and full of supply, not only attractive to people but also able to build them up.

THE WAY TO BEAR FRUIT

Concerning the way to bear fruit, first you should set aside three hours every week to contact your acquaintances for the preaching of the gospel. If you are willing to do this, every month you will baptize one person. After that person is baptized, you should immediately give him a lesson concerning the way of life. The lesson does not need to be too long; the important thing is to tell him that the Lord is the processed Triune God, that He died on the cross for our redemption and resurrected to become the life-giving Spirit, and that now He is in the spirit of those who call on His name, to be their life and reality. At any time we can turn to Him from deep within, call on His holy name, and pray to Him. Whenever we encounter some problem or need in our living, we should immediately call on Him. After you finish the lesson, you should lead him to practice, and you can demonstrate so that he can see what you are doing, and also ask him to demonstrate for you, until he learns how to do it.

Besides this, you should tell him that we Christians not only need to pray but also need to read the Bible. First, you must tell him that from that night on, every night before he goes to bed he should read one chapter of the New Testament, and that this will help him to have a pleasant sleep and will also benefit him in the long run. Next, you should teach him how to pray-read. Then ask him to have morning revival with you over the phone for ten minutes, beginning the next day, that by doing this he can contact and enjoy the Lord. Do not read too many verses each time; to read just two or three verses is good enough. Not only so, you should also visit him every three or more days. In the first month of his baptism, it is best for you to visit him seven or eight times, to have face-to-face fellowship with him, to minister life to him, and to give him some proper proposals and definite guidance. Not long after this, you will be able to see that he is growing in the Lord and has changed; thus, he will have become stable.

During the same period of time, after he is saved, you should bring him to a group meeting. In the group meeting, the main thing is to do the work of perfecting; it is best to spend half the time to do this work. You can use the verses for the morning revival as the content, and everyone can open his mouth to share and fellowship what he has received during the week. Those who are more experienced can fellowship some deeper points; if some make errors in their sharing, the experienced ones should exercise wisdom to make adjustments. Then, unconsciously the truth will be released, and the attendants will spontaneously be nurtured and edified.

EXERCISING THE LORD'S AUTHORITY

Another point is that when we preach the gospel, we not only can go to knock on "warm doors," but we can also bring our relatives, friends, colleagues, and classmates to the group meeting. In the meeting, we should not greet them in a conventional way or converse with them regarding mundane matters; rather, we should exercise the Lord's authority and act according to the Lord's command, leading them to believe, be baptized, and be saved. We must believe that whatever we do in the Lord's name will count. Matthew 28:18-19 tells us that the Lord has received all authority in heaven and on earth, and He commanded us to go to disciple the nations, baptizing them into the name of the Father, the Son, and the Spirit. Therefore, we should not be afraid; we simply need to say by faith, "Today Jesus Christ commands you to believe in Him." If they say that they do not know how to believe, we should lead them to pray and call on the Lord's name; then we should say to them that to call on the Lord is to be saved. After this we should tell them to be baptized immediately. We should never think that we need to speak until they are clear and then lead them to be baptized. It is the Lord who regenerates people; it is not time that regenerates. First, we baptize people into the Triune God; then we teach them what the Lord commanded us (Matt. 28:20).

The practice of the new way requires that we be slow and steady like a stream. The more I study it, the more I feel we cannot be too hurried or too quick. However, we should know that the Lord will fulfill these Scriptures in us. We must look to the Lord's mercy to lead us completely into these things.

(A message given by Brother Witness Lee in Kuching, Malaysia on November 1, 1990)

CHAPTER THREE

THE RECOVERY OF THE GOD-ORDAINED WAY

(2)

Scripture Reading: Eph. 1:10; 3:9-10

THE WORSHIP THAT GOD DESIRES TO HAVE

In the Old Testament, in the age prior to Moses, the worship and service to God were all rendered individually, as can be seen in men such as Adam, Abel, and Enosh. But after Moses, they were rendered corporately. God delivered the children of Israel out of Egypt through Moses that they might become a kingdom of priests (Exo. 19:6). From that time on, the worship that God desires of His people has no longer been individual but corporate. God did not annul the individual worship, but the individual worship is not the goal that God desires to obtain. God's eternal plan, or economy, is to have a corporate worship. It is not to have many corporate worships separately; rather, it is to have one great, universal, corporate worship among tens of thousands of God's people. From the time of Moses, this kind of worship continued for fifteen or sixteen hundred years among the children of Israel.

In the Old Testament the worship rendered to God by His people was formed according to the Mosaic law. That corporate worship was merely an empty shell; it was short of the content of reality. It developed to the extent that the worship of the children of Israel had only a name but did not have the reality, and it fell altogether into outward forms. Thus, it lost the presence of God, even God Himself, the One who was the real content and center of their worship. All their actions in worshipping God were not only vanity but were even detested by God.

In the New Testament we see in the Lord Jesus and in His forerunner, John the Baptist, that the worship that God desires is beyond our imagination, for it is altogether not a matter of formality. The Jews who studied the Old Testament all knew that the Messiah would come and that prior to His coming His forerunner, Elijah, would come to pave the way for Him. However, when Christ and His forerunner came, the Jews did not recognize them. Although the Jews expected the Messiah to come according to the Old Testament prophecies, they interpreted the Scriptures in letters and in forms, and thus they were mistaken and missed Him.

John the Baptist was the Elijah promised by God in the Old Testament (Matt. 11:14). At his conception, it was spoken concerning him that he would go before the Lord in the spirit and power of Elijah (Luke 1:17). He was born into a priestly family; his father Zachariah was a priest who took the lead in his course of priestly service. According to what was ordained by the law, John was to inherit his father's priesthood and serve in the holy temple, wear the priestly robe, and eat the priestly food. However, when he grew up and began his ministry, what he did was altogether different. He put on a garment of camel's hair and wore a leather girdle about his loins, and he ate locusts and wild honey. All these things are uncivilized, uncultured, and contrary to the religious regulations. He altogether abandoned God's Old Testament dispensation, which had fallen into a kind of religion mixed with human culture. His intention was to introduce God's New Testament economy.

In Christ we also see something extraordinary. When Christ was born, although the priests and scribes had the knowledge concerning the birth of Christ, they did not see the vision, nor did they have the heart to seek after Christ; thus, they missed Him and did not gain Him. Although the Bible knowledge they had was accurate, it was in dead letters. This calls to mind the situation of Christianity. Christianity preaches Christ, but it has deviated in its preaching of Christ, having only the name of Christ but not the reality. What is left is nothing but an empty shell, void of Christ as the content. As early as the third or fourth century, Constantine the Great of Rome adopted Christianity as the state religion, and from that point on, the "church" became detached from Christ. It became something in name only, without Christ as its content, something that is mixed with the world. Christ in His ascension is altogether heavenly, yet the "church" on the earth is separated from Christ.

THE RAISING UP OF THE LORD'S RECOVERY

I must point out to you that today both Christianity and Catholicism have become greatly deformed. The reason is that some use the name of Christ, but they put Christ aside. This is a counterfeit. Many things that are not of God are mixed in. The result is something half true and half false. Because of this, the Lord raised up His recovery among us. In 1922 He began His work of recovery in the Far East; and then it proceeded to Taiwan, to Southeast Asia, to East Asia, to the United States, and now it has spread to the six continents of the whole world. You who are present here have also received the Lord's mercy and have come into the Lord's recovery. I hope you realize that you should not compare the Lord's recovery with today's Catholicism or Protestantism because it is different.

At the beginning of this meeting I read to you two portions of the Scriptures, Ephesians 1:10 and 3:9-10. Both portions mention one thing, that is, the dispensation of the mystery of God. The Bible shows us that God has an eternal heart's desire, and according to His heart's desire, He designed a plan, had a counsel, and made an arrangement. This plan, this counsel, this arrangement, is the economy that we often speak of. In brief, the economy of God is that God desires to have a group of people, who were created according to His image, that He may be their life and everything and that He may build them up as a corporate vessel, the church, which is the Body of Christ, the bride of Christ, the house of God, and the kingdom of God, for the fulfillment of God's goal.

Based on this, God desires that every saved person, every believer as a member of Christ, who has the life of Christ and the Spirit of Christ, should be living, organic, and full of function. If we compare this with the condition in today's Catholicism or Protestantism, we know that it is altogether different. Among them they have brought forth a clerical class, with a few members of the clergy replacing the organic functions of the majority of the laity. This is contrary to the biblical teaching, and it should be condemned. For this reason God wants to recover the way that He ordained.

Although we say that we are in the Lord's recovery, a good part of what we have, we inherited from Catholicism and Protestantism. Because of this, it has not been easy for us to break away from these things. We came out from that kind of background. A considerable part of our way of meeting and of preaching the gospel was inherited from them. A principle with all of these inherited ways is that they require only a few people and do not require everyone to function. Therefore, we may say that in our standing, we are the Lord's recovery, but in our practice, a great part of what we are is not the Lord's recovery because some of our ways have killed the functions of many members of the Body of Christ. When we speak of church service, we refer mainly to the participation by the brothers and sisters in practical affairs; those who participate in the spiritual aspect of the service are very few.

THE RECOVERY OF THE GOD-ORDAINED WAY

According to the revelation in the Bible, the gospel preaching that the Lord desires is that every saint should go personally to contact people and to preach the gospel to save sinners. But, fairly speaking, up to the present, the gospel preaching among us has not gone back to the way taught in the Bible. The Lord's Word tells us that every disciple of the Lord should preach the gospel (Matt. 28:19), and every branch of the Lord should bear fruit (John 15:5, 16), and even bear remaining fruit. For this reason, the Lord also wants us to feed His lambs (John 21:15), to nourish the regenerated believers with the riches of the Lord's life. To do this requires us first to set aside a definite time every week to visit our acquaintances to bring God's salvation to them. If we do this every week, in a year we will surely be able to baptize several people. Then, we need to take care of them and feed them regularly. If we truly mean business to do this, I have the assurance that every one of us will be able to bring two yearly into the church life. This is a great thing.

Furthermore, the Bible requires us to perfect the saints that they may do the work of the New Testament ministry to build up the Body of Christ (Eph. 4:12). This should not be done by just a few; it requires every part of the Body to perfect one another, and the best place to do this is in the group meetings. In the group meetings the saints can understand one another, and if there is any problem or need they can pray for one another. Furthermore, the mutual fellowship issues in mutual feeding and mutual help. In addition, there is mutual discussing of the truth. We have found a very good way, that is, to take one of the books of the Bible as a line and pray-read two or three verses every day in sequence. Then, when we come to the group meetings, we have more than ten verses that we can bring out for mutual sharing and for discussing together. After we have done this for a period of time, we will be well-nourished in the truths of the Bible. We believe that God will recover this condition among us everywhere.

After the preaching of the gospel, the feeding of the lambs, and the perfecting of the saints, we have the final item, which is to prophesy for the building up of the church. To prophesy is to speak to men building up, encouragement, and consolation (1 Cor. 14:3); it is not merely to predict. Every one of us who comes to the meeting should have something that he prepared beforehand. We should bring what we have received of the Lord in our daily life and offer it. You speak something, and I speak something; this will edify people and glorify God.

Up to the present time, these four things—everyone preaching the gospel, feeding the lambs, perfecting the saints, and prophesying to build up the church—have not been fully recovered among us. Since these things are in the Bible, God will recover them. These things are rare in Christianity; but since we are here as the Lord's recovery, we need to rise up quickly and press on to endeavor and strive in these four things. We should not be content with our condition. We are not rich in content; especially in these four things we are weak and are not strong enough, and we are old and not fresh enough. Hence, we need to be revived every morning and overcome every day. Furthermore, we must determine to endeavor to learn in the God-ordained way. As long as we are willing to learn, nothing will be impossible.

ENDEAVORING TO LEARN

My burden is here: Brothers, the Bible shows us that God has an economy in which He wants to have a corporate vessel, the church, the ultimate consummation of which is the New Jerusalem. Therefore, the situation that will be in the New Jerusalem should be the condition of the church on earth today. However, when we look at the situation in Catholicism and in Protestantism, and then look at our condition, we see that the entire situation is deficient and does not resemble what it should be, and falls behind what is written in the Word of God. If the Lord cannot gain us, He will go to gain others. Sooner or later the Lord will gain a group of people through whom His holy Word can be fully recovered. His heart's desire must be fulfilled and His economy must be accomplished.

Furthermore, according to the entire world situation, it seems that the Lord is quickly doing this very thing; He is speeding up His recovery. I hope that all the saints in Southeast Asia can also see the light of this revelation and practice and learn with dedication. I do not mean that you should immediately do this and do that; you just need to be willing to do these things and to learn, practicing them step by step in earnestness. You do not need to stir up everyone to do them together; that may not be effective. The best way is to take the lead yourself. First, two or three may take the lead to do these things, then gradually there may be five or six, then eight or nine, and so on. In this way, spontaneously there will be an atmosphere in the church in which everyone is preaching the gospel, feeding the lambs, perfecting the saints, thereby directly participating in the building up, in knowing the truth, in growing in life, and prophesying in the meetings for the building up of the church. As a result, the recovery of the God-ordained way will be widespread; every saint will be filled with the life of Christ and the Spirit of Christ, and everyone will be living, organic, and functioning. This is the true revival of the church, and it is also the real situation of recovery that the Lord desires to have. May the Lord have mercy on us.

(A message given by Brother Witness Lee in Kuching, Malaysia on November 2, 1990)

Chapter Four

THE NEW TESTAMENT PRIESTLY SERVICE

(1)

Scripture Reading: Rev. 1:5-6; Rom. 15:16; 1 Pet. 2:5, 9; Eph. 3:2; 1 Cor. 9:16-17; Eph. 3:8; John 15:16; Psa. 119:147-148; Rom. 8:37; Eph. 5:18b; 2 Tim. 4:2a; John 21:15; 1 Thes. 2:7; Eph. 4:11-12; Heb. 10:24-25; 1 Thes. 2:11

OUTLINE

I. All the New Testament believers being priests to serve God—Rev. 1:5-6.

II. The priests of the gospel of God—Rom. 15:16:

  A. Being built up into God's holy priesthood—the whole church becoming the New Testament priesthood of the gospel—1 Pet. 2:5a.

  B. Telling out the virtues (such as love, grace, and forgiveness) of the One who has saved us out of darkness into His marvelous light—1 Pet. 2:9.

  C. Carrying out the stewardship of the grace of God in God's economy—Eph. 3:2; 1 Cor. 9:16-17.

  D. Ministering to others the unsearchable riches of Christ as the grace of God—Eph. 3:8.

  E. Offering up spiritual sacrifices acceptable to God, that is, offering up the saved sinners as members of Christ to constitute the Body of Christ—1 Pet. 2:5; Rom. 15:16b.

  F. Being chosen and appointed by God to bear remaining fruit—John 15:16.

G. The living of the priests of the gospel of God:
1. Being revived every morning—Psa. 119:147-148.
2. Overcoming every day—Rom. 8:37.
3. Being filled with the Spirit every moment—
   Eph. 5:18b.
4. Speaking Christ everywhere—2 Tim. 4:2a.

III. Feeding the lambs in the Lord's flock—John 21:15:
A. Through the home meetings in the new believers'
   homes.
B. As a nursing mother would cherish her own
   babes—1 Thes. 2:7.

IV. Perfecting the saints—Eph. 4:11-12:
A. Through the group meetings:
1. Not a religious service.
2. Not a Bible-study meeting.
3. But the Christians' own assembling—for considering one another, inciting one another to love
   and good works, and exhorting one another—
   Heb. 10:24-25.
B. Bringing the new believers who are under our
   nourishing to attend the group meetings.
C. Besides the mutual fellowship, intercession, care,
   shepherding, and testifying, the main thing in the
   group meetings being to teach one another that all
   may be perfected.
D. Entreating and consoling the believers and testifying to them as a father to his own children—
   1 Thes. 2:11.

In this message we will see the New Testament priestly service ordained by God.

ALL THE NEW TESTAMENT BELIEVERS
BEING PRIESTS TO SERVE GOD

The New Testament service ordained by God in the Scriptures indicates that all New Testament believers are priests to serve God (Rev. 1:5-6). The priests are those who serve God. Everyone who serves God, anywhere and at any time, must be a priest whose special profession is to serve full time before God. Although he serves full time, he still labors for his livelihood, working with his own hands to minister to his own needs. Paul was the top and best serving one of God in the New Testament. He also held the job of tent-making, laboring and working with his own hands. He not only ministered to his own needs but also took care of the needs of his co-workers. Therefore, on the one hand, we serve God exclusively, and on the other hand, we also have a way to make a living. We should not allow others to worry about us because of our serving the Lord.

THE PRIESTS
OF THE GOSPEL OF GOD

Almost everywhere in the entire New Testament, God speaks concerning how to be priests of the gospel of God, how to serve God. Paul called the New Testament priests the priests of the gospel (Rom. 15:16). They are priests, yet they are gospel preachers, priests who specialize in the gospel. In the Old Testament the priests specialized in taking care of the sacrifices. By this we can see that the priests of the gospel, mentioned in Romans 15:16, are those who specialize in taking care of the gospel. In Greek, the phrase *a priest of the gospel* has a further meaning; it denotes not only a priest of the gospel, but a laboring priest of the gospel. In other words, the New Testament priests of the gospel should be laboring priests of the gospel—not priests who are content or at leisure, but priests diligently striving and laboring. They are priests who diligently labor in the gospel of God. Paul was such a priest of the gospel of God, and we too should be such.

Being Built Up into God's Holy Priesthood

According to the New Testament, there are at least seven aspects related to being priests of the gospel of God. First, these priests are built up into God's holy priesthood. The priests of the gospel of God do not serve alone or individually; they are built up into a priesthood. We know that today any kind of successful work in human society must be a work that is carried out by an organized group. It is difficult for individuals to have a great success; the achieving of a great success depends on the effort of an organized group. The priests in the Old Testament did not serve individually; they carried out their duty group by group. They all belonged to the house of Aaron; they were sons of Aaron formed into a body of priests. Luke chapter one tells us that when Zachariah the priest went to serve God, he served in the priestly body according to the order of his course. When we preach the gospel in the church today, we also should realize that the whole church constitutes a priesthood of the gospel.

In Greek, one word is used for *priestly duties* or *priestly work* and another for *priestly body* or *priesthood,* but in English the two words are treated as one. Therefore, in reading the English Bible, it is often difficult to tell what the particular word denotes. What is referred to both in 1 Peter 2:5 and 9 is the priesthood, not the priestly duties. Today in the church, we, the priests of the gospel, should be built up together to serve in coordination as a body of priests. Do not consider this a small thing. If we preach the gospel without any building up, but in a very individualistic way, our gospel will never be powerful or effective. For the preaching of the gospel to be both powerful and effective, we must be built up together and coordinated together.

In church history it is difficult to find one Christian body that has not been divided. It is not easy for us to be coordinated and built up in the church, for although we have been regenerated in our spirit, we often do not speak or walk in our spirit. If we want the church of the Lord to be blessed, first we must learn the lesson of coordination.

We should learn to be upright and not crooked, to obey the Lord, and to be built up with others into a holy priesthood.

Telling Out the Virtues of the One Who Has Saved Us out of Darkness into His Marvelous Light

Second, the priesthood of the gospel should tell out the virtues (such as love, grace, and forgiveness) of the One who has saved us out of darkness into His marvelous light (1 Pet. 2:9). To tell out His virtues is to tell out what He is in His attributes. Our telling out to people in this way is our preaching of the gospel. To be the priests of the gospel of God is to tell out the virtues of what He is, to tell out how He has saved us out of darkness into His marvelous light.

Carrying Out the Stewardship of the Grace of God in God's Economy

Third, the priests of the gospel of God should carry out the stewardship of the grace of God in God's economy (Eph. 3:2; 1 Cor. 9:16-17). As the New Testament priests of the gospel, we have a stewardship, and our stewardship is the economy of God. Every time we go out to preach the gospel, we are carrying out our stewardship in God's economy to dispense Christ's salvation and life to others.

Ministering to Others the Unsearchable Riches of Christ as the Grace of God

Fourth, the priests of the gospel should minister to others the unsearchable riches of Christ as the grace of God. This is to dispense Christ to people.

Offering Up Spiritual Sacrifices Acceptable to God, That Is, Offering Up the Saved Sinners as Members of Christ

Fifth, after we dispense Christ to others, there will be a result. Others will receive and believe in the Lord, and we will baptize them into the Triune God. Thus, the sinners whom we save become the spiritual sacrifices that we can offer up to God for His acceptance, and they also become members of

Christ to constitute the Body of Christ (1 Pet. 2:5; Rom. 15:16b). After a sinner is saved and baptized through us, he becomes a lamb of the Lord to be offered as a sacrifice to God, and he also becomes a member of the Body of Christ to constitute the Body of Christ.

As priests, we must offer sacrifices. All the sacrifices of the Old Testament are types of Christ. Therefore, what the Old Testament priests offered were types of Christ; we may say that they offered Christ in type. But what the New Testament priests offer is Christ Himself, because the sinners whom we save are members of the Body of Christ, and they thereby constitute the Body of Christ. Therefore, in God's eyes what we, the New Testament priests of the gospel, offer is Christ. In the Old Testament, what was offered were types of the individual Christ, whereas in the New Testament what is offered is the reality of the corporate Christ. Therefore, what we offer is more and higher than what was offered in the Old Testament. Whenever we gain one person by preaching the gospel, we should rejoicingly offer him on the altar as a sacrifice to God and as a member of Christ's Body. When all the members are added together, they constitute the Body of Christ. Therefore, what we offer is the corporate Christ.

Being Chosen and Appointed by God
to Bear Remaining Fruit

Sixth, we have been chosen and appointed by God to bear remaining fruit (John 15:16). It is not difficult to bear fruit, but to bear remaining fruit requires effort. At the time of fruit bearing, a farmer must be busier than in ordinary times. For example, he must prevent the birds from coming to eat the fruit. In like manner, to bring forth children is easy, but to nurture them is difficult. According to my observation, the number of baptized ones among us is not small; there are many baptized ones everywhere. However, at the end of the year, when we take a count, not many remain. The reason is that after people are baptized, there is a lack of care and there is not much nourishing. For this reason, after people are saved, we need to spend time to nourish them and to care for them. If we do this, after half a year or a year, they will be solidly in the church.

The Living of the Priests of the Gospel of God

Being Revived Every Morning

In order that we may be the New Testament priests of the gospel, we must have a living that matches our priesthood. To be a certain kind of people, we must have a certain kind of living. To be the priests of the gospel, we must have the living of the priests of the gospel. First, we need to be revived every morning. Psalm 119:147 says, "I prevented the dawning of the morning, and cried: I hoped in thy word." Morning is the beginning of a day; in the morning everything is fresh. If we desire to enjoy the Lord's fresh supply, like the psalmist, we need to rise early to call on the Lord and to look to His word—to eat, drink, and enjoy Him through His word. You do not need to spend too much time or read too many verses; two or three verses a day are sufficient. At the same time, do not skip in your reading. Rather, read book by book. The best way is to start with the books that are easy. Books such as the Gospel of John, Romans, Galatians, and Philippians are very good material for morning revival. Read two or three verses every morning. Then, on Saturday go back to review the verses for the previous five days, and try to put your impressions and feelings together and arrange them so that they become the contents of your prophesying in the Lord's Day meeting.

Overcoming Every Day

As the priests of the gospel of God, we need not only to be revived every morning but also to overcome every day. Romans 8:37 says, "But in all these things we more than conquer through Him who loved us." Although Paul encountered many problems in his experience, he could always give thanks to God because he had found the secret. In his living he adopted an overcoming attitude with an overcoming standing. We also should be like this in our living. Regardless of what happens, we should have an overcoming faith, take an overcoming attitude, and stand on the position of the Lord's victory to boast to our environment.

Being Filled with the Spirit Every Moment and Speaking Christ Everywhere

To be revived every morning and to overcome every day has become our motto in all the churches around the globe today. As priests of the gospel, we must have this kind of living. Not only so, we need to be filled with the Spirit every moment (Eph. 5:18b) and to speak Christ everywhere (2 Tim. 4:2a). This truly is the most beautiful and best living in the world.

FEEDING THE LAMBS IN THE LORD'S FLOCK

What we spoke previously concerns the preaching of the gospel to save sinners, which is also what we call begetting. This is the first step. The second step is nourishing. After the begetting, there is the need of nourishing. We all know the story in John 21. The disciples were not able to catch any fish the entire night. Then the Lord came to perform a miracle, enabling them to catch a net full of fish, and He also prepared breakfast for them. After breakfast, the Lord said to Peter, "Do you love Me more than these?" Peter said, "Yes, Lord, You know that I love You." The Lord said, "Feed My lambs" (John 21:15). Of the four Gospels, the first three—Matthew, Mark, and Luke—charge us at the end to preach the gospel; only the Gospel of John charges us to feed the Lord's lambs. Chapter fifteen says that we should bear remaining fruit, and chapter twenty-one says that we need to feed the lambs. Every one of us should not only preach the gospel to save sinners, but also should have two or three lambs in our hands.

The best way to feed the lambs is through the home meetings in the new believers' homes. To ask the new believers to come to our homes is not as good as our going to their homes. This kind of feeding will enable the new believers to remain. When we take care of and nourish the new believers, we should be like a nursing mother cherishing her own babes (1 Thes. 2:7), not only feeding them but also caring intimately for them that they may be comforted and encouraged and may feel happy. This can be accomplished through the help of praying together, singing hymns, and reading the Word.

PERFECTING THE SAINTS

The third step is to perfect the saints, that is, to teach them (Eph. 4:11-12), which is usually carried out through the group meetings. If we lead people to salvation and feed them as lambs, we may bring them together to form a group meeting. The group meeting is not a religious service; it is the manifestation of the Christian living. It does not have a set way. Rather, it is free and informal. While we are on the way to the meeting, we should call on the Lord's name and sing hymns. No one knows when the meeting begins. There are no regulations, and there is no one who takes the lead. Everyone simply lives together, and spontaneously there is fellowship, intercession, knowing the need of one another, and care for one another. Furthermore, this kind of group meeting is not a Bible-study with someone teaching and presiding over the meeting. Rather, it is a meeting for everyone to share and testify, to ask questions if they so desire, and to answer according to each one's own knowledge and experience. Through this, everyone will receive the teaching and the help in truth and in life.

This kind of group meeting is the Christians' "own" assembling as mentioned in Hebrews 10, which is for considering one another, inciting one another to love and good works, and exhorting one another (vv. 24-25). Therefore, we need to bring the new believers who are under our nourishing to attend this kind of group meeting. Besides the mutual fellowship, intercession, care, shepherding, and testifying, the main thing in the group meetings is to teach one another that all may be perfected. For this reason, we need to entreat and console the believers and to testify to them as a father to his own children (1 Thes. 2:11).

The final step is to prophesy for God, which we will cover in the next message.

The words I have presented before you are all according to the Scriptures. Therefore, this is the New Testament service ordained by God. I hope that you will bring this word to the Lord to pray much and to look to Him. May the Lord have mercy on us.

(A message given by Brother Witness Lee in Petaling Jaya, Malaysia on November 6, 1990)

CHAPTER FIVE

THE NEW TESTAMENT PRIESTLY SERVICE

(2)

Scripture Reading: 1 Cor. 14:3, 12, 4-5, 1, 39a, 31, 23-25

OUTLINE

V. Prophesying for God:
  A. Being not predicting.
  B. But speaking to men:
    1. Building up (for the church)—1 Cor. 14:3.
    2. Encouragement (for the work)—1 Cor. 14:3.
    3. Consolation (for the believers)—1 Cor. 14:3.
  C. Being the excelling gift—1 Cor. 14:12.
  D. Being for the building up of the church—1 Cor. 14:4-5, 12.
  E. In the larger church meetings.
  F. Concerning prophesying for God, the believers:
    1. Needing to pursue and desire earnestly—1 Cor. 14:1, 39a.
    2. Needing to learn—1 Cor. 14:31.
    3. All having the capacity—1 Cor. 14:31.
    4. All having the obligation—1 Cor. 14:23-25.

PROPHESYING FOR GOD

In this message we will cover the fourth step of being a priest of the New Testament, that is, prophesying for God.

The preaching of the gospel is for begetting, that is, for regenerating people. The feeding of the lambs is for nourishing, that is, for cherishing the babes. The perfecting of the saints is for teaching, that is, for instructing people in the truth. Prophesying for God is for building, that is, for the building up of the church.

Speaking may be considered the greatest ability or skill. We may speak the same word, yet you may speak it in one way and I in another way. Hence, there needs to be much consideration in this matter. In the New Testament, there is one chapter, 1 Corinthians 14, that is altogether concerned with the matter of prophesying. The Greek word that is rendered *prophesy* in this chapter may also be rendered *predict*. However, whichever way we may render it, both prophesying and predicting are not to speak for ourselves but to speak for God. We must keep this point firmly in mind. When we prophesy in the church, we speak for God and not for ourselves. God is our source; He is the word that we speak. When we prophesy for God, we speak for God, speak forth God, and speak God into people to dispense God to them.

In 1 Corinthians 14 Paul spoke altogether about prophesying. He highly exalted prophesying and greatly belittled speaking in tongues. He said, "Greater is he who prophesies than he who speaks in tongues, unless he interprets, that the church may receive building up" (1 Cor. 14:5). He also said, "But in the church I would rather speak five words with my mind that I might instruct others also, than ten thousand words in a tongue" (1 Cor. 14:19). For this reason, he encouraged us again and again to prophesy for God.

Being Not Predicting

To prophesy for God is not to predict. To predict is to foretell an event before it occurs. This is not the meaning conveyed in 1 Corinthians 14. The Chinese Union Version renders this word "to be a prophet preaching." However, the term *prophet* may lead people to understand the Greek word here as referring to predicting. Actually, what the prophets of God spoke in the Old Testament did not altogether consist of predictions; rather, their speaking included a great measure of exhortations and warnings. In 1 Corinthians 14, in speaking of prophesying for God, Paul did not have any intention for us to speak in tongues or to predict; his intention was that we all speak for God. God desires to speak to His people. However, He would not speak directly to them; He wants us to speak for Him. Therefore, this matter is very precious, and for this reason it is also quite difficult.

But Speaking to Men Building Up, Encouragement, and Consolation

First Corinthians 14:3 says, "But he who prophesies speaks to men building up and encouragement and consolation." Building up is for the church; the church needs the words of building up. Exhortation is for the work; the Lord's work needs the words of exhortation. Consolation is for the believers; every believer needs the words of consolation, because every day we all have problems and worries, and we all need to be consoled. Therefore, when we prophesy for God in the church meetings, we first need to take care of the building of the church of God, that the church may be built up. Second, we need to take care of the Lord's work. Because they have many problems, everyone who works for the Lord needs incitement and encouragement. Third, we also need to take care of all God's children that they may have joy and satisfaction. Therefore, we should remember that to prophesy is to speak building up for the church, to speak encouragement for the work, and to speak consolation for the believers.

Being the Excelling Gift

First Corinthians 14:12 says, "Since you are zealous of spirits, seek that you may excel for the building up of the church." Speaking in tongues is for the building up of ourselves; thus, it is a gift of lesser value. Only prophesying is for the building up of the church; thus, it is the excelling gift. How transcendent and noble it is if we can speak for God by speaking some illuminating words that everyone may be comforted and may be full of joy and hope, and that the church may be built up.

Being for the Building Up of the Church

Prophesying is the excelling gift because it builds up the church (1 Cor. 14:4-5, 12). Prophesying not only builds up individual saints, but also builds up the Body of Christ, which is the church.

In the Larger Church Meetings

Because there are more people in the larger meetings, the words that we prophesy are more powerful.

Concerning Prophesying for God, the Believers:

Needing to Pursue and Desire Earnestly

First Corinthians 14:1 says, "Pursue love, and desire earnestly spiritual gifts, but rather that you may prophesy." We need to desire earnestly the most profitable gift, which is the gift of prophesying. Since to prophesy for God is to speak for God and to speak forth God, it is to minister Christ to people. This is the most important thing in the church meetings and the most profitable gift in the building up of the saints and the church. In the concluding word of this chapter, Paul still charged us to pursue and desire earnestly to prophesy for God's building (v. 39).

Needing to Learn

First Corinthians 14:31 says, "For you can all prophesy one by one, that all may learn and all be encouraged." God's desire is that every believer would prophesy. For this reason, we should not only earnestly desire this gift but also make an effort to learn and exercise.

All Having the Capacity

Every saint has the capacity to prophesy for God. God has given this gift to us. All believers possess this gift, and all can prophesy for God.

All Having the Obligation

First Corinthians 14:23-25 shows us if all prophesy in the church meetings, this will cause people to be convicted and to be brought back to God. However, if we do not prophesy, we owe God something, we owe others something, and we even owe ourselves something. In the church meetings, the thing that edifies people the most is prophesying. Furthermore, what we prophesy edifies ourselves the most. If in a meeting you stand up to prophesy for God, you feel that that meeting is good; otherwise, you may not feel that it is good. Actually, whether a meeting is good or not does not depend on the meeting itself, but on whether or not you prophesy for God. The reason is that once you speak, the meeting is yours, and all the riches become your supply. Therefore, if we want to be blessed and edified, we should pray and prophesy in the meetings. This is our duty to God and man.

That God wants us to speak for Him is based on the principle of incarnation. Under the grace of the New Testament, God does not want to do things by Himself; He wants man to cooperate with Him. God and man, man and God, coordinate mutually and cooperate together. When we speak, God speaks. This truly benefits man and glorifies God. Therefore, I encourage all of you to prophesy for God. Do not be afraid or be shy. One who is shy cannot learn to speak a foreign language well. The same is true with our prophesying for God. Do not be afraid; regardless of this or that, speak and keep speaking. Do not be afraid that people will laugh at you if do not speak well. The more you speak, the more you will be able to speak. Furthermore, we can learn from one another and teach one another. We all are students and we all are teachers. Consequently, we all are being perfected and are becoming good prophets.

If we do mean business to learn to prophesy, I would propose to you that every week you set aside two hours and come together with eight or ten to teach one another and to learn from one another. For this reason, every one of you should have a morning revival every day. There is a publication that is very suitable for this, *The Holy Word for Morning Revival,* which contains Scripture text, portions from footnotes, and portions from Life-study messages for our pray-reading and enjoyment of the Lord every morning. When you have a morning revival every day in this way, you will surely have some inspiration which you may jot down. When the weekend comes, you may put together the portions that you have written down, read them over, and do a little polishing so that it will be approximately three minutes long. This becomes a very good draft for your prophesying. Doing this is something very basic, and it will be of great benefit to you.

Furthermore, in order to prophesy for God, we need to know more of the Bible. Therefore, we need to memorize the best Scripture verses. If you learn to memorize one or two verses a day, you will have an accumulation of the Word. Then, unconsciously, your prophesying will be strengthened. In addition, when you prophesy, avoid wordiness or common words; instead, speak God's word and speak concise words. Eight or ten of you may take turns to practice, to adjust one another, and to learn from one another. Within half a year or a year you will do very well. At that time, when you come together, you will be able to speak for God; you will be able to speak to the point and speak with substance. Furthermore, you will be able to speak forth God so that people can understand, and you will be able to speak God into people so that they can receive the benefit. If in a meeting twenty people can prophesy in this way, no individual preaching can compare with their speaking. When you practice this, in the beginning it may not be so good, but that does not matter. We should simply encourage everyone to speak. It does not matter if we have to "sacrifice" the meeting somewhat. After some practice, gradually the proper condition will be manifested and the improper condition will disappear. After you have learned to prophesy and the ability has been developed, you will receive great profit. Not only will you be able to speak in the meetings, but even your speaking in your daily life will be helped.

We receive the inspiration in our daily life, and then we can present it in the meetings for the building up of the church. Therefore, our prophesying is not our instant inspiration; it is to prepare something from what we have received of the Lord in our daily life and to offer it in the meetings for others' benefit and for the church's building up. I put these words before you. As long as you mean business to practice this, I am confident that you all will be able to prophesy for God and become New Testament priests of the gospel who fulfill their responsibility.

(A message given by Brother Witness Lee in Petaling Jaya, Malaysia on November 6, 1990)

CHAPTER SIX

THE PROPHECIES
CONCERNING CHRIST'S COMING
AND CONCERNING
THE CONSUMMATION OF THE AGE

Scripture Reading: Dan. 9:24-27; Matt. 24:3, 15, 21, 27, 32-33, 36-42; Luke 21:34-36; Rev. 3:10; 1 Thes. 4:16-17; 2 Thes. 2:3-4, 8; 2 Pet. 1:19

OUTLINE

I. Seventy weeks being apportioned out by God—Dan. 9:24-27.

II. The signs of Christ's coming and of the consummation of the age—Matt. 24:3:
   A. The great tribulation—Matt. 24:21; Luke 21:34-36; Rev. 3:10.
   B. Antichrist—Matt. 24:15; 2 Thes. 2:3-4, 8.
   C. The fig tree—Matt. 24:32-33.
   D. The rapture of the saints—Matt. 24:36-42; 1 Thes. 4:16-17; Matt. 24:27.

III. Giving heed to the prophetic word—2 Pet. 1:19.

In this message I will fellowship with you about the prophecy concerning Christ's coming and concerning the consummation of the present age. This may be considered my favorite subject from the time I was saved to the present time, a period of more than sixty years.

SEVENTY WEEKS BEING APPORTIONED OUT BY GOD

When we speak concerning Christ's coming, we cannot avoid speaking concerning the consummation of the present age. The age we are in today is the age of grace. Before this age there was the age of the law, beginning with Moses' decreeing of the law and continuing for approximately one thousand five hundred years. At the first coming of Christ, the age of the law was terminated. Christ brought grace and reality, and on the cross He accomplished God's redemption. Thus the age of grace began. The age of grace is the age of the church; it is also called the age of mysteries. This age began with Christ's first coming, and it will end with Christ's second coming. When Christ comes back, He will conclude this age and bring in the kingdom age. The conclusion, the consummation, of this age is not something that takes place in one day. According to the revelation of the Bible, it will be at least seven years long. Therefore, if we want to understand Christ's coming back, we must have a clear understanding concerning the last seven years of the present age. These seven years are not recorded in the New Testament; they are recorded in Daniel 9:24-27. These four verses tell us a great key point, which is also a secret.

At this point, we will first mention the background in which the book of Daniel was written. At about 606 B.C., Nebuchadnezzar, the king of Babylon, conquered Jerusalem and carried away all the children of Israel as captives, among whom was Daniel. At that time Daniel was a youth in his teens. He loved God and feared God, and for God's holy city and holy temple he humbled himself before God, praying and giving thanks to God three times a day. At the time when the seventy years of Israel's captivity were about to be completed, he understood by the books that contained the word of God to Jeremiah that the number of years determined by God for the accomplishing of the desolation of Jerusalem was seventy years. Therefore, he sought God by prayer and supplications, with fasting and sackcloth and ashes. God sent an angel to speak to Daniel: "Seventy weeks are apportioned out for your people and for your holy city, to close transgression, to make an end of sins, to make propitiation for iniquity, to bring in the righteousness of the ages, to seal up vision and prophet, and to anoint the most holy place" (Dan. 9:24, new translation).

The seventy weeks were divided into three sections. The first section consists of seven weeks, counting from the twentieth year of King Artaxerxes (Neh. 2:1-8). First, King Cyrus defeated Babylon, and, moved by God, he made a proclamation that all the children of Israel should go back to rebuild the holy temple; then, Artaxerxes issued a decree for the rebuilding of Jerusalem. The period from the issuing of the decree to restore and rebuild Jerusalem to the completion of the restoration and rebuilding was a total of forty-nine years. Thus Jerusalem was built again with street and moat (Dan. 9:25). The second section of the seventy weeks consists of sixty-two weeks, from the completion of the rebuilding of Jerusalem to the cutting off of the anointed One (Messiah— Christ), a total of four hundred thirty-four years. In that very year, the four hundred thirty-fourth year, on the fourteenth day of the first month, the day of the Passover, the Lord Jesus was crucified. At a later time, the people of the prince who will come will destroy the city and the sanctuary; and the end of it will be with a flood, and even to the end there will be war; the desolations are determined (Dan. 9:26). Thus, the first section plus the second section equals sixty-nine weeks.

At this point the seventy weeks were interrupted. A long period of time would follow before the last week would come. It is not possible to find out the length of this interval. This interval is the age of the church, which is the age of grace. It is also called the age of mysteries. This age begins and ends with the two comings of Christ. In this age, everything that God did, is doing, and will do is a mystery. For example, Christ's incarnation, His crucifixion, His resurrection, and His becoming the Spirit to enter into His believers that they may be formed into the church as the members of His Body are all mysteries. Although today we come from different places and speak with different accents, we have the same Christ dwelling in us to make us one. This is a mystery. Not only is Christ a mystery, but also the church is a mystery. Although we are different in our birth, in our nationality, in the color of our skin, and in our race, we pursue the same Lord, and we are co-witnesses of Christ. Furthermore, one day we will be transfigured together to meet before the Lord. These are the mysteries that have been hidden from the ages, but at the sounding of the seventh trumpet, at the consummation of the present age, all these mysteries will be finished and concluded, and everything will become open and manifest (Rev. 10:7).

When will this age come to an end? When will the last week come? The Bible clearly reveals that at the beginning of the last week, Antichrist will make a firm covenant with Israel for seven years; in the middle of the seven years he will break the covenant, terminate Israel's sacrifices and oblations to God, and persecute those who fear God (Dan. 9:27; Rev. 12:13-17). He will set up the idol of abomination in the temple to replace God, and he will carry out a great destruction to cause desolation (Matt. 24:15) until Christ comes to the earth. Then Christ will slay Antichrist by the breath of His mouth and bring Antichrist to nothing by the manifestation of His coming (2 Thes. 2:8; Rev. 19:19-20). According to the plain words and the revelation in the Bible, the coming of the last week is related to the following few things: Antichrist and the restored Roman Empire, the restoration of Israel (including the rebuilding of the temple), the great tribulation, and the rapture of the saints.

ANTICHRIST

Matthew 24:3 says, "And as He sat on the Mount of Olives, the disciples came to Him privately, saying, Tell us,...what is the sign of Your coming and of the consummation of the age?" In His reply in the succeeding verses, the Lord first spoke concerning Antichrist. In verse 15 the Lord said: "When therefore you see the abomination of desolation, spoken of through Daniel the prophet, standing in the holy place (let him who reads understand)." This will definitely be fulfilled in the last three and a half years of the present age, the time of the great tribulation, the second half of the last week. At that time Antichrist's image will be set up as an idol in the temple of God.

In 2 Thessalonians 2:3-4 Paul also said, "Let no one deceive you in any way; because it will not come unless the apostasy comes first and the man of lawlessness is revealed, the son of destruction, who opposes and exalts himself above all that is called God or an object of worship, so that he seats himself in the temple of God, proclaiming himself that he is God." This shows us that before the consummation of the age, Antichrist must first appear; he will play a leading role in the last week.

Revelation 13:1 points out that a beast, which signifies Antichrist, will come up out of the Mediterranean Sea. This beast has seven heads and ten horns. Revelation 17:8-11 tells us the origin of this beast. The seven heads of the beast are seven Caesars of the Roman Empire. According to historical records, the Roman Empire had a total of twelve Caesars, but only six of them were referred to in Revelation, because all these six were "fallen" (Rev. 17:10 and note); that is, they all died unnaturally—they either committed suicide or were murdered, their throne being usurped. Antichrist, the seventh Caesar, will come from one of the Gentile nations around the Mediterranean Sea. He will have the support of ten kings, and they will unite to form a great empire, which will be the revived Roman Empire. He will make a covenant with Israel for seven years and permit them to freely worship God. After three and a half years, Antichrist will be slain temporarily; then the spirit of the fifth Caesar (Nero) of the Roman Empire will come up out of the abyss and enter into the dead body of Antichrist to resurrect him to be the eighth Caesar. Antichrist will break the covenant and begin to persecute the Israelites and the Christians. He will also set up his image in the temple (Matt. 24:15; 2 Thes. 2:4), until the complete destruction that is determined will be poured out upon the desolator, that is, upon Antichrist (Dan. 9:27).

Antichrist will be the Caesar of the revived Roman Empire. Once he makes a seven-year covenant with Israel, that will be the beginning of the last week. Today, this last week is not yet manifested because the Roman Empire is not yet revived; but as we observe the world situation, it seems that the restoration of the Roman Empire will take place soon. In the previous two years we all have seen the great change in the world situation, a change that is beyond our imagination. First, the Soviet Union is proceeding with a reformation and has declared her renunciation of communism. Then a number of her satellite countries have risen up to copy her action. Now East Germany and West Germany are unified. Thus, the entire situation in Europe is pushing toward the direction prophesied in the Bible for the restoration of the Roman Empire. When that time comes, Antichrist will appear.

THE RESTORATION OF ISRAEL

In Matthew 24 the Lord gave a clear revelation concerning the restoration of Israel. In verse 32 the Lord said, "But learn the parable from the fig tree: when its branch has already become tender and puts forth its leaves, you know that the summer is near." To the saints, the fig tree is a sign of the consummation of the age. In Matthew 21:19, during His last visit to Jerusalem, the Lord Jesus cursed a fig tree because He could not find any fruit on it. The fig tree is a symbol of the nation of Israel (Jer. 24:2, 5, 8). Because Israel was stubborn and rebellious and had no fruit that could satisfy God, she was rejected by God. In A.D. 70, Titus, the Roman prince, brought with him a great army to destroy Jerusalem and the temple, as prophesied by the Lord when He said, "A stone shall by no means be left upon a stone which shall not be thrown down" (Matt. 24:2). From that time, the children of Israel were scattered among the nations. Not only did their nation fall, but even their homeland was lost. Humanly speaking, there was truly no hope for the nation of Israel to be reformed. However, the Bible contains a prophecy saying that one day the cursed and dried up fig tree would become tender and put forth leaves.

When I was newly saved, shortly after the end of World War I, many books concerning Bible prophecy were published. After studying the prophecies, I had doubts in my heart, wondering how it could be possible for the nation of Israel to be reformed. The Holy Land belonged altogether to the Arabs, and the site of the temple had been occupied for seven centuries. However, since this prophecy is the word in the Bible, I dared not be unbelieving. In 1948 I was working in Shanghai. One day the newspaper carried a report on the front page: the nation of Israel had been restored! When I heard the news, I almost jumped up in great excitement. The fig tree truly had "become tender." Then, after another nineteen years, in 1967, during the six-day war, Israel seized Jerusalem; that was the fig tree "putting forth leaves." At that time I was even more excited. I knew that the summer was near, right at the door; it would not be long before the full restoration of the nation of Israel would take place.

THE REBUILDING OF THE TEMPLE

Concerning the rebuilding of the temple, first we need to see the two halves of the last week. The last week will be cut into two halves by Antichrist's abolishing of the seven-year covenant he will make with Israel. In the first three and a half years, Antichrist will support the children of Israel, permitting them to freely worship God; in the latter three and a half years, Antichrist will cause the sacrifice and the oblation to cease (Dan. 12:7; 9:27) and replace them with an idol of himself. In Matthew 24:15, the holy place in which Antichrist's image will stand refers to the sanctuary within the temple (Psa. 68:35; Ezek. 7:24; 21:2) and the abomination refers to the image of Antichrist as an idol. In other words, the idol will remain in the temple for three and a half years until Christ will destroy Antichrist by the manifestation of His coming. Therefore, first the temple will have to be rebuilt; then the children of Israel will be able to worship God and offer sacrifices to Him, and Antichrist will be able to set up his image.

Since A.D. 70, when Titus destroyed the temple, the temple has never been rebuilt. Israel has regained Jerusalem and is actively making preparations for the rebuilding of the temple.

All the materials that will be needed for the rebuilding of the temple and all the utensils needed for the sacrifices have been prepared according to what is recorded in the Bible. Now they are waiting for the suitable time to come, and the rebuilding of the temple will be completed.

THE GREAT TRIBULATION

The second half of the last week, the last three and a half years of this age, is the period of the great tribulation, such as has not occurred from the beginning of the world until now, nor ever shall be (Matt. 24:21). This period will begin with the supernatural calamities in the sixth seal of the seven seals (Rev. 6:12-17) and will end at the seventh bowl of the seven bowls (Rev. 16:1-21). It will be "the hour of trial which is about to come on the whole inhabited earth, to try them who dwell on the earth" (Rev. 3:10). This great tribulation will come from three directions—from God, from Antichrist, and from Satan—upon all those dwelling on the face of all the earth (Luke 21:35). At that time God will judge the entire universe with supernatural calamities, so that the earth will not be suitable for man's existence. It seems that God will say to the men on earth, "I created all things for your existence, and My purpose is that you would fear Me, serve Me, love Me, and pursue after Me; yet you cooperate with Satan to oppose Me and reject Me. Now I am shaking the earth and the heavens; see if you will still be able to live peacefully." Furthermore, Satan will be cast out of heaven to the earth by the overcomers, and knowing that he has a short time, he will collaborate with Antichrist, and the two will do their best to destroy and injure the human race, and they will severely persecute the Jews and the Christians (Rev. 12:7-13, 17). However, for the preservation of His people, God will limit the time of the great tribulation to only three and a half years; otherwise, no flesh would be saved.

THE RAPTURE OF THE SAINTS

Before the great tribulation, the overcomers will be raptured, leaving the majority of the believers, those who are not yet mature, on the earth to pass through the great tribulation. Matthew 24:40-41 says, "Then shall two men be in the field; one is taken, and one is left. Two women shall be grinding at the mill; one is taken, and one is left." This indicates that while the worldly people are befuddled by material things, with no sense of the coming judgment, some of the sober and watchful believers will be taken away. To the befuddled and senseless people, this should be a sign of Christ's coming. Therefore, we should take heed to ourselves, lest at some time our hearts be weighed down with debauchery and drunkenness and the anxieties of life (Luke 21:34), and we miss the rapture and become like Lot's wife.

At that time, the earth will become a place that is terribly unsuitable for man's living. The supernatural calamities and Antichrist's persecution will cause the believers on earth to suffer great afflictions; but God will keep and nourish them (Rev. 12:14). At the end of the great tribulation, the majority of the believers, including the resurrected ones and the remaining ones, will be raptured to the air (1 Thes. 4:16-17) at the Lord's coming (*parousia*). Then, Christ will suddenly appear in an open way to the earth, like the flashing of lightning (Matt. 24:27).

These are the signs of Christ's coming and of the consummation of the age. Although concerning that day and hour no one knows (Matt. 24:36), the year can be figured out. Before the consummation of this age, Antichrist will come out to be the Caesar of the revived Roman Empire. He will make a seven-year covenant with the children of Israel, and that will be the beginning of the last week. Thus, if anyone should say, "Behold, here is the Christ!" or, "There is the Christ!" we will not be deceived (Matt. 24:23). However, neither should we become slothful, thinking that, since the Lord is delaying His coming, we can eat and drink and become drunken (Matt. 24:48-49). We need to be watchful and ready that we may prevail to escape all these things which are about to take place, and to stand before the Son of Man (Luke 21:36).

GIVING HEED TO THE PROPHETIC WORD

After we have seen and are clear about all these prophecies, we need to be watchful and to give heed to the prophetic word as to a lamp shining in a dark place, until the day dawns and the morning star rises in our hearts (2 Pet. 1:19). Prior to His open appearing as the sun, the Lord will appear as the morning star in the darkest hour of the night to those who are longing for His appearing. The prophetic word of the Scripture, as the shining lamp to the believers, conveys spiritual light to shine in their darkness, guiding them to enter into a bright day until the day of the Lord's appearing.

The time is short. By studying the prophecies in the Bible and checking with the world situation today, we know that the day of the Lord's coming is very near and that the last week is approaching. The crucial question today is this: Do we want to bury ourselves in the world or put ourselves in the Lord's hand? We should know that once we bury ourselves in the world and become rooted in it, it will not be easy to be uprooted. In the few remaining days, we should get ourselves ready. Let us be those who love and serve the Lord, who are revived and are overcoming every day, and who let the world go and are waiting with all our heart for the Lord's coming.

(A message given by Brother Witness Lee in Kuching, Malaysia on October 30, 1990)

CHAPTER SEVEN

THE BELIEVERS' ATTITUDE
TOWARD THE COMING OF CHRIST

Scripture Reading: Rev. 12:5; 14:1; Luke 21:36; 1 Thes. 4:16-17; 2 Thes. 2:8; 2 Tim. 4:8; Phil. 3:20b-21; 2 Tim. 4:1; Matt. 24:42-44; 25:13

OUTLINE

I. The coming—*parousia* (presence)—of Christ:
   A. Beginning from the heavens before the great tribulation—Rev. 12:5; 14:1; Luke 21:36.
   B. Coming down to the air toward the end of the great tribulation—1 Thes. 4:16-17.
   C. Coming to the earth at the conclusion of the great tribulation—2 Thes. 2:8.
II. The believers' attitude toward the coming of Christ:
   A. Loving it—2 Tim. 4:8.
   B. Awaiting it—Phil. 3:20b.
   C. Taking it as an encouragement—2 Tim. 4:1.
   D. Watching and being ready for it—Matt. 24:42-44; 25:13.
   E. Beseeching to prevail—Luke 21:36.

THE UNFOLDING OF THE PROPHECIES
CONCERNING CHRIST'S SECOND COMING

In the period before the Reformation, the Catholic Church paid little attention to the second coming of Christ. After the Reformation, the Christians in the Protestant churches began to pay attention to the prophecies concerning this matter and brought them out one by one. After the early apostles passed away, the church on earth had great problems, especially in arguments related to the expounding of the Bible, so that eventually the church was divided into two parts, the Eastern church and the Western church. Consequently, in A.D. 325 Emperor Constantine of Rome called a council at Nicea. All the Christian leaders assembled together and formulated the Nicene Creed, which temporarily settled all their arguments. Then, after another two hundred years, in A.D. 590, the papal system was formally established and was universally recognized by the church. This became the Roman Catholic Church.

Under the rule of the Catholic Church, the church passed through a period called the Dark Ages for ten centuries. Then in 1517 Martin Luther took the lead to reform the church, and he translated the Bible into German, thus opening up the biblical truths. After this many Protestant groups were formed, and different items of the truth were gradually released. However, the truth concerning the Lord's second coming remained vague. Then in 1828 the brothers in England were raised up by the Lord. They were enlightened by the Lord concerning the truth, and there was a great advancement in the knowledge of the Bible. In a general way, under their hand the prophecies concerning the Lord's second coming were crystalized. In particular, J. N. Darby made the greatest contribution. However, the logic in his line of thought was somewhat deficient, and the details regarding the Lord's second coming were not made sufficiently clear. Later, the Lord raised up G. H. Pember, who was well versed in biblical prophecy, especially in the history of the prophecies. He wrote four books concerning the prophecies of the Bible. One of them, entitled *The Great Prophecies,* covers the prophecies concerning the Jews, the Gentiles, and the church; the other three also cover the prophecies concerning the Jews, the Gentiles, and the church, respectively. These four books may be considered the foundation of the study of biblical prophecy. Everyone who pursues the knowledge of the prophecies in the Bible is helped by these four books. Pember was well versed in the history of the biblical prophecies, and his study in this matter was excellent. For example, concerning the vision of the struggle between the ram and the he-goat in Daniel 8, Pember realized that the he-goat signifies the Grecian Empire, and the ram, the Persian Empire, because the symbol of ancient Greece was the goat, and the symbol of Persia was the ram.

If we trace the history in the Old Testament, we see that God raised up Gentile powers to chastise Israel because of Israel's rebellion. First, God raised up Chaldea, also known as Babylon. In 606 B.C. Nebuchadnezzar, the king of Babylon, led a great army to destroy the holy city, Jerusalem, and the holy temple, and he brought all the children of Israel as captives to Babylon. However, because Nebuchadnezzar was too cruel toward the children of Israel, seventy years after Israel's captivity, God raised up the empire of Medo-Persia. From the book of Isaiah we can see that Cyrus, the king of Persia, was God's beloved, and he even became a type of Christ. In 539 B.C. Cyrus defeated Babylon and, under God's inspiration, released the children of Israel that they might go back to rebuild the temple. This is recorded in the book of Ezra. Then, after another four kings, King Artaxerxes gave the order for the rebuilding of the city of Jerusalem. This is recorded in the book of Nehemiah. Therefore, for a period of time Persia was doing the will of God. At approximately 330 B.C., Alexander rose to power in Macedonia, north of Greece. When he was in his thirties he formed the Grecian Empire, and within a short time he conquered the land east of the Mediterranean all the way to the Indian Ocean. Thus he defeated Persia, symbolized by the ram. When he invaded Jerusalem, the high priest Jaddua went to meet him and showed him the portion in Daniel concerning the he-goat. After reading it, Alexander had great appreciation for it, so he began to treat the Jews with leniency. He had strength like that of a goat and was brutal and high-handed. History records that when he returned to Macedonia, he wore a crown with a he-goat's horn.

After Pember came Robert Govett, who wrote concerning the biblical prophecies with the greatest accuracy. Later, his student D. M. Panton published a magazine entitled *Dawn,* in which he released a number of truths concerning prophecy. He gave financial assistance to M. E. Barber, enabling her to come to mainland China. M. E. Barber originally came with a British mission to Foochow, China to do missionary work. Later, because of some false accusations, she was called back to England. After the storm calmed down, she withdrew from the mission and received the burden from the Lord to come back to China. At that time the Lord raised up Brother Watchman Nee in Foochow. Brother Nee not only learned many precious spiritual lessons from Miss Barber, but also through her recommendation came in contact with the writings of Panton and others.

In 1928 in Shanghai, Brother Nee had a Bible study on the book of Revelation, and he gave me a draft of the notes when I joined the Lord's work in 1933. Then in 1976, in Anaheim, California, I held a training on the Life-study of Revelation. Today in the Recovery Version of the New Testament, the notes related to the prophecies are extracts obtained through my study of the writings of Darby, Pember, Govett, Panton, and Brother Nee. These notes are very clear and transparent. Hence, our knowledge concerning the biblical prophecies has a solid foundation; it did not come out of our own imagination, nor is it our original, unique creation. Rather, what we see is an advancement that we made by standing on the shoulders of those who were before us.

By studying the writings of these Bible scholars, we have concluded that, in the past two hundred years, if those who have expounded the prophecies concerning the Lord's second coming made any mistakes, their mistakes were on two points. The first point is related to the last week of the seventy weeks in Daniel, and the second is related to the coming of Christ and the rapture of the saints. In expounding the prophecies, anyone who neglects the last of the seventy weeks will fall into error. In the past some said that Napoleon was the Antichrist. However, Napoleon was a French king, and in his time the nation of Israel was not yet restored. In the 1930s, Panton said that Mussolini was the Antichrist, and he published the pictures of Nero and Mussolini, pointing out the resemblance between the two. Later, others said that Hitler was Antichrist. However, Antichrist will be resuscitated after being slain, but Hitler's body was not even intact for burial after his death. Recently, there has been a great change in the Middle East situation, and some have predicted that Iraq's President Hussein will be the Antichrist. However, Hussein is an Arab, but Antichrist will come out of one of the nations around the Mediterranean Sea. All these sayings are wrong and are not in accordance with the prophecy concerning the last week.

THE COMING—*PAROUSIA* (PRESENCE)—OF CHRIST

Now we will speak concerning the coming—*parousia*—of Christ. The Greek word *parousia* means *presence;* in ancient times it was applied to the coming of a dignified person. In the New Testament this word refers to the coming of Christ, the presence of the most dignified One. This presence will last for a period of time. It will begin first in heaven with the rapture of the overcomers before the three and a half years of the great tribulation (Rev. 12:5; 14:1; Luke 21:36); then, toward the end of the great tribulation, it will come down and remain in the air (1 Thes. 4:16-17); finally, at the conclusion of the great tribulation, it will come from the air to the earth (2 Thes. 2:8).

The Rapture of the Saints

As far as the overcomers are concerned, the rapture of the saints to Christ's presence will take place before the great tribulation, but as far as the majority of the saints are concerned, it will occur on the last day of the great tribulation. Before the great tribulation, the man-child will be caught up to the presence of Christ in the heavens where the throne of God is (Rev. 12:5). The firstfruit also will be raptured to the presence of Christ in the heavens, where the heavenly Mount Zion is (Rev. 14:1-4). In addition, the other overcomers who are living at that time will be raptured to the presence of Christ in the heavens and will stand before Him (Matt. 24:40-41; Luke 21:36; Rev. 3:10) to enjoy the Lord's presence and escape the great tribulation.

The majority of the believers, those who are not raptured before the great tribulation, will be left to pass through the great tribulation so that they may reach maturity. During that period of time, there will be numerous supernatural calamities, and Antichrist will do all he can to cruelly oppress the saints. As a result, the world will no longer be a lovable place. Although they will experience God's care and nourishing, the believers will still be miserable. Then, at the completion of the three and a half years, at the sounding of the last trumpet, all the dead saints throughout the generations will be resurrected and, together with the living saints who remain, will be raptured to the presence of Christ in the air (1 Thes. 4:15-17; 1 Cor. 15:51-52). This will include the rapture of the ten resurrected virgins (Matt. 25:1-12) and the rapture of the two witnesses, who will be resurrected (Rev. 11:11-12). At that time the Lord will set up His judgment-seat to judge all the saints (2 Cor. 5:10), and He will also marry His overcomers who will be invited to the wedding feast of the Lamb as the bride of Christ (Rev. 19:7-9). After that, Christ will appear openly.

The Destruction of Antichrist

After the wedding feast of the Lamb, Christ will come with His overcomers, His newlywed wife, as His army to fight with Antichrist, the kings under him, and their armies at Armageddon (Rev. 16:14, 16). At that time, the armies of Antichrist will gather there for war to destroy the nation of Israel. There Christ will tread the great winepress of God's wrath (Rev. 14:19), and the blood will reach to the bridles of the horses (Rev. 14:20). Because of His treading, Christ's garment will be dipped in blood (Rev. 19:13). On the one hand, Christ will bring Antichrist to nothing by the manifestation of His coming (2 Thes. 2:8); on the other hand, like lightning, He will appear to the children of Israel, and the whole house of Israel will be saved (Matt. 24:27, 30; Rev. 1:7; Rom. 11:26-27; Zech. 12:10-14). After this, Christ will send an angel to bind Satan and cast him into the abyss (Rev. 20:1-3). Thus He will bring His kingdom to the earth (Rev. 11:15; 12:10a). He will sit on His throne of glory to judge the nations who are living at that time and separate them from one another. The "sheep," those who obey the eternal gospel and who treat the suffering believers well, will be blessed and be counted righteous to inherit the kingdom; but the "goats," those who disobey the eternal gospel, will be cursed and will suffer eternal perdition (Matt. 25:31-46; Acts 10:42b; 2 Tim. 4:1).

The Restoration of Israel

During the great tribulation, Israel will be trampled under foot by Antichrist and his army (Rev. 11:2). Furthermore, the principal calamities of the great tribulation will occur in that land (Matt. 24:16-22). At the end, Antichrist will kill many of the Jews and will besiege them on the Mount of Olives. However, at the very moment of peril, Christ will come on the clouds of heaven with power and great glory, and all Israel will look to the One whom they pierced, and they will wail for Him and repent (Matt. 24:30; Zech. 12:10). Then Christ will descend onto the Mount of Olives to save Israel (Zech. 14:4-5). After Christ judges the nations, He will send His angels with a loud trumpet, and they will gather together from the four winds all the children of Israel to the good land which He promised to Abraham. That will be the time of the restoration of the nation of Israel (Matt. 24:31), and it will usher in the restoration of all things (Acts 3:21). At that point, the kingdom age will begin.

THE BELIEVERS' ATTITUDE
TOWARD THE COMING OF CHRIST

Loving It, Awaiting It, and
Taking It as an Encouragement

Since we know that the Lord's second coming is so precious, we should love the Lord's appearing (2 Tim. 4:8). The Bible concludes with "Come, Lord Jesus!" (Rev. 22:20).

From the record in the New Testament, it is not difficult to discover that in their hearts the apostles firmly believed that the Lord would come quickly, and they also lived a life in preparation for the Lord's second coming. In the church's history, I know that Miss M. E. Barber was one who lived such a life. On the last day of 1925, Brother Nee went to pray with her, and she prayed, "Lord, do You really mean to say that You will let 1925 pass by, that You will wait until 1926 before You come back? However, on this last day I still pray that You will come back today!" Not long afterwards, Brother Nee met her on the street, and again she said to him, "It is really strange that up to this day He has not yet come back." Do not think that since we are clear concerning the signs of the Lord's coming, we can be slothful and can first love the world and then pursue the Lord when the last week comes. There is no such convenience. We should believe that the Lord is to be feared. In Luke 12 the Lord gave a parable concerning a rich man who endeavored to lay up wealth for himself so that his soul might enjoy itself and be merry. But God said to him, "Senseless one, this night they are requiring your soul from you" (vv. 16-20). Every "today" that we have is truly the Lord's grace. Therefore, as long as we have today, as long as we still have breath, we should love the Lord and His appearing, await the Lord's coming (Phil. 3:20), and always take His coming as an encouragement.

In 2 Timothy 4:1 Paul said to Timothy, "I solemnly charge you before God and Christ Jesus, who is about to judge the living and the dead, and by His appearing and His kingdom." This is an exhortation from Paul immediately before his martyrdom. He said that he had fought the good fight, he had finished the course, and he had kept the faith, and that at the judgment seat he would be awarded the crown of righteousness, which would be awarded to all those who have loved His appearing (2 Tim. 4:6-8). He reminded Timothy, and also us, by the Lord's judgment and kingdom that we should have a living that loves the Lord's appearing. This will cause us not to be discouraged, not to backslide, not to become weak, but to remain faithful to the end.

Watching and Being Ready for It

When the Lord comes, He will come secretly as a thief to those who love Him, and will steal them away as His treasures and bring them into His presence in the heavens (Matt. 24:42-43). Hence, we need to watch and be ready (Matt. 25:13; 24:44). If we desire to be raptured, first we must be filled with the heavenly breath and have oil in our vessels. If we are rooted on the earth and occupied daily with the anxieties of this life and with earthly pleasures, we will not be raptured at that time. We should remember Lot's wife. Because she loved and treasured the evil world which God was going to judge and utterly destroy, she took a backward look. Thus, she became a pillar of salt and was left to suffer in a place of shame. This should be a warning to us. If we love the world, the Lord will leave us here to pass through the great tribulation that we may be put to shame until we become mature and are raptured.

Beseeching to Prevail

The Lord also reminded us to take heed to ourselves and to be watchful, at every time beseeching, lest our hearts be weighed down with dissipation (or debauchery) and drunkenness and anxieties of life, and that the day of the great tribulation come upon us suddenly as a snare; for it will come in upon all those dwelling on the face of all the earth. We should guard our hearts and give all the room to the Lord that we may prevail to escape all these things and to stand before the Son of Man (Luke 21:34-36; cf. Rev. 12:5-6, 14).

To attain maturity is not an overnight matter. Therefore, for His coming we must prepare ourselves, love Him, and grow in Him, that at His appearing we may be mature to be raptured and receive the reward.

(A message given by Brother Witness Lee in Kuching, Malaysia on October 31, 1990)

ABOUT THE AUTHOR

Witness Lee was born in 1905 in northern China and raised in a Christian family. At age 19 he was fully captured for Christ and immediately consecrated himself to preach the gospel for the rest of his life. Early in his service, he met Watchman Nee, a renowned preacher, teacher, and writer. Witness Lee labored together with Watchman Nee under his direction. In 1934 Watchman Nee entrusted Witness Lee with the responsibility for his publication operation, called the Shanghai Gospel Bookroom.

Prior to the Communist takeover in 1949, Witness Lee was sent by Watchman Nee and his other co-workers to Taiwan to ensure that the things delivered to them by the Lord would not be lost. Watchman Nee instructed Witness Lee to continue the former's publishing operation abroad as the Taiwan Gospel Bookroom, which has been publicly recognized as the publisher of Watchman Nee's works outside China. Witness Lee's work in Taiwan manifested the Lord's abundant blessing. From a mere 350 believers, newly fled from the mainland, the churches in Taiwan grew to 20,000 in five years.

In 1962 Witness Lee felt led of the Lord to come to the United States, and he began to minister in Los Angeles. During his 35 years of service in the U.S., he ministered in weekly meetings and weekend conferences, delivering several thousand spoken messages. Much of his speaking has since been published as over 400 titles. Many of these have been translated into over fourteen languages. He gave his last public conference in February 1997 at the age of 91.

He leaves behind a prolific presentation of the truth in the Bible. His major work, *Life-study of the Bible,* comprises over 25,000 pages of commentary on every book of the Bible from the perspective of the believers' enjoyment and experience of God's divine life in Christ through the Holy Spirit. Witness Lee was the chief editor of a new translation of the New Testament into Chinese called the Recovery Version and directed the translation of the same into English. The Recovery Version also appears in a number of other languages. He provided an extensive body of footnotes, outlines, and spiritual cross references. A radio broadcast of his messages can be heard on Christian radio stations in the United States. In 1965 Witness Lee founded Living Stream Ministry, a non-profit corporation, located in Anaheim, California, which officially presents his and Watchman Nee's ministry.

Witness Lee's ministry emphasizes the experience of Christ as life and the practical oneness of the believers as the Body of Christ. Stressing the importance of attending to both these matters, he led the churches under his care to grow in Christian life and function. He was unbending in his conviction that God's goal is not narrow sectarianism but the Body of Christ. In time, believers began to meet simply as the church in their localities in response to this conviction. In recent years a number of new churches have been raised up in Russia and in many European countries.

OTHER BOOKS PUBLISHED BY
Living Stream Ministry

Titles by Witness Lee:

Abraham—Called by God	978-0-7363-0359-0
The Experience of Life	978-0-87083-417-2
The Knowledge of Life	978-0-87083-419-6
The Tree of Life	978-0-87083-300-7
The Economy of God	978-0-87083-415-8
The Divine Economy	978-0-87083-268-0
God's New Testament Economy	978-0-87083-199-7
The World Situation and God's Move	978-0-87083-092-1
Christ vs. Religion	978-0-87083-010-5
The All-inclusive Christ	978-0-87083-020-4
Gospel Outlines	978-0-87083-039-6
Character	978-0-87083-322-9
The Secret of Experiencing Christ	978-0-87083-227-7
The Life and Way for the Practice of the Church Life	978-0-87083-785-2
The Basic Revelation in the Holy Scriptures	978-0-87083-105-8
The Crucial Revelation of Life in the Scriptures	978-0-87083-372-4
The Spirit with Our Spirit	978-0-87083-798-2
Christ as the Reality	978-0-87083-047-1
The Central Line of the Divine Revelation	978-0-87083-960-3
The Full Knowledge of the Word of God	978-0-87083-289-5
Watchman Nee—A Seer of the Divine Revelation ...	978-0-87083-625-1

Titles by Watchman Nee:

How to Study the Bible	978-0-7363-0407-8
God's Overcomers	978-0-7363-0433-7
The New Covenant	978-0-7363-0088-9
The Spiritual Man • 3 volumes	978-0-7363-0269-2
Authority and Submission	978-0-7363-0185-5
The Overcoming Life	978-1-57593-817-2
The Glorious Church	978-0-87083-745-6
The Prayer Ministry of the Church	978-0-87083-860-6
The Breaking of the Outer Man and the Release ...	978-1-57593-955-1
The Mystery of Christ	978-1-57593-954-4
The God of Abraham, Isaac, and Jacob	978-0-87083-932-0
The Song of Songs	978-0-87083-872-9
The Gospel of God • 2 volumes	978-1-57593-953-7
The Normal Christian Church Life	978-0-87083-027-3
The Character of the Lord's Worker	978-1-57593-322-1
The Normal Christian Faith	978-0-87083-748-7
Watchman Nee's Testimony	978-0-87083-051-8

Available at
Christian bookstores, or contact Living Stream Ministry
2431 W. La Palma Ave. • Anaheim, CA 92801
1-800-549-5164 • www.livingstream.com